The Story of a Special Day
Volume 54

February

23

The 54ᵗʰ day of the year. There are 311 days (312 in leap years) remaining until the end of the year.

by Michael Dobson

Timespinner
Press

This book is also available in e-book form for Kindle, e-pub devices, and other formats from your favorite online booksellers.

For more information about the series, about us, or about your special day, please email us at editor@timespinnerpress.com.

Look for other volumes in *The Story of a Special Day*, coming often. See www.timespinnerpress.com for details and for the most recent information.

Table of Contents

For the definition of "O.S.," "N.S.," "CE," and "BCE" used with some dates , see the section "On Names and Dates."

Cover: Official US Navy photograph titled "First Iwo Jima Flag Raising. Small flag carried ashore by the 2d Battalion, 28th Marines is planted atop Mount Suribachi at 1020, 23 February 1945," by SSGT Louis R. Lowery, USMC staff photographer for *Leatherneck* magazine — for the EVENT OF THE DAY.

Quote of the Day

"The cost of liberty is less than the price of repression."

W. E. B. Du Bois, civil rights activist and educator
born February 23, 1868

Today in History

February 23

The Stars and Stripes atop Mount Suribachi, Iwo Jima (Photo: John Papsun)

Event of the Day
Raising the Flag on Iwo Jima

The Battle of Iwo Jima, in which US Marines captured the island from the Japanese Imperial Army during World War II, took place from February 19 to March 26, 1945, and involved some of the bloodiest fighting in the Pacific Theater. Four days into the conflict, on February 23, 1945, the Marines captured Mount Suribachi, depriving the Japanese of a key observation point.

The First Flag

On the morning of February 23, Lieutenant Harold Schrier led the 40-man Third Platoon, Easy Company, 2nd Battalion, 28th Marines, to seize and occupy the crest of the mountain. Before the climb, the battalion commander gave Lieutenant Schrier the flag from their transport ship, saying, "If you get to the top, put it up."

The platoon encountered little resistance, and after a 2½ climb reached the top around 10:15 in the morning. Turning a length of Japanese iron water pipe found on the mountaintop into an improvised flagpole, Schrier and two Marines fastened the flag to the pole and planted it atop the mountain.

The flag was clearly visible to Marines and sailors on the beachhead and on nearby ships, and a loud cheer broke out. Ships blasted their horns in celebration. All the noise alerted the Japanese, who then began firing on the flagstaff, but to no avail.

1

Marine Staff Sergeant Louis Lowery, a photographer with *Leatherneck* magazine, who had accompanied the platoon, took the photograph of the flag raising that you see on the cover of this book.

Marines climbing Mount Suribachi carrying a US flag

The Second Flag

Accompanying the American invading force was the Secretary of the Navy, James Forrestal. Now that the beachhead was reasonably secure, he decided to go ashore in the company of the Marine Corps commander, General Holland "Howlin' Mad" Smith. Looking at the small American flag high atop the mountain, Forrestal decided that he wanted that flag as a souvenir.

The 2nd Battalion commander, Colonel Chandler Johnson, was not amused. "To hell with that!" he said. The flag, after all, was the property of his battalion. Instead, he sent his operations officer back to the beach to obtain a replacement flag. "And make it a bigger one!" he added.

A large flag was found, and a small team of Marines, accompanied by Associated Press photographer Joe Rosenthal, climbed the mountain with the new flag. As the Marine platoon attached the new flag to the water pipe, Rosenthal began to pile up rocks to give himself a higher platform from which to take photographs.

Rosenthal nearly missed the famous shot. "Out of the corner of my eye, I had seen the men start the flag up," he said in a later interview, "I swung my camera and shot the scene. That is how the picture was taken, and when you take a picture like that, you don't come away saying you got a great shot. You don't know."

Returning to the beach following the flag-raising, Rosenthal sent his film to Guam for processing. The AP photo editor immediately recognized the importance of the photograph, and rushed it into print.

"Raising the Flag on Iwo Jima" (Photo: Joe Rosenthal, Associated Press.)

It was picked up by hundreds of newspapers throughout the United States, and Rosenthal was later awarded the Pulitzer Prize for Photography.

After he took the famous photograph, Rosenthal took additional photographs, including several posed shots, leading to later claims that the "Raising the Flag" photo was itself staged. Motion picture film taken during the raising of the flag shows that this was not the case.

The Bond Tour

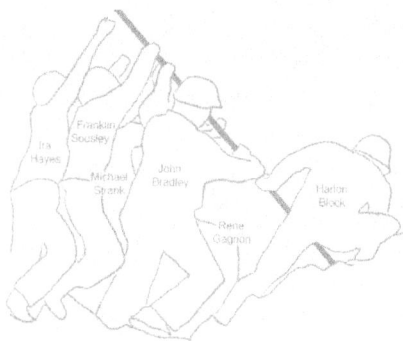

Outline of the figures at the flag raising, by Jeff Dahl CC BY-SA 4.0

Of the six Marines in the photograph, three (Michael Strank, Franklin Sousley, and Harlon Block) were killed on Iwo Jima. Meanwhile, in Washington, President Franklin D. Roosevelt decided that the soon-to-be iconic photograph would make a great symbol for an upcoming War Loan campaign, and ordered the surviving flag-raisers brought back to the US following the battle.

There was some difficulty identifying the people in the photograph. Flag-raiser Ira Hayes did not wish to be identified. Harlon Block, one of the casualties during the battle, was misidentified as Sgt.

Hank Hansen, who had also been killed in the battle, an error not corrected until 1949. Navy Corpsman John Bradley, was mistakenly identified in place of PFC Harold Schultz, and it wasn't until 2016 that the correct identification was made. (Bradley, who received the Navy Cross for heroism for braving enemy fire to rescue a wounded Marine, had participated in the first flag raising but not in the Rosenthal photograph.)

Two surviving flag raisers, Ira Hayes and Rene Gagnon, along with supposed third flag-raiser John Bradley, were sent on a nationwide tour. Hayes, who had not wanted to be identified, had drinking problems during the tour and was ordered back to duty a number of weeks before the tour ended. However, the war bond drive was a great success, raising over $26 billion (over $350 billion in 2016 dollars), twice its original goal.

The Legacy

The photograph has become one of the iconic images of the Second World War. Sculptor Felix de Weldon used it as the model for the US Marine Corps Memorial in Alexandria, Virginia. Both Iwo Jima flags, from the first and second flag raisings, can be found in the collection of the National Museum of the Marine Corps in Quantico, Virginia.

Ira Hayes, suffering from survivor guilt, depression, and alcoholism, died at the age of 32. His story was told in the 1961 motion picture *The Outsider*, with Tony Curtis as Hayes. A folk song,

"The Ballad of Ira Hayes," was recorded by Johnny Cash in 1964, and later covered by Bob Dylan.

James Bradley, the son of John Bradley, chronicled the story in his 2000 best-seller *Flags of Our Fathers*, later made into a 2006 film directed by Clint Eastwood.

Poster for the 7th War Loan Drive (1945)

A U.S. Marine Corps ceremonial bugler, standing on monument, plays taps as an honor guard presents the colors during the Sunset Parade June 5, 2012, at the Marine Corps War Memorial in Arlington, Va. (Photo: Lance Cpl. Tia Dufour)

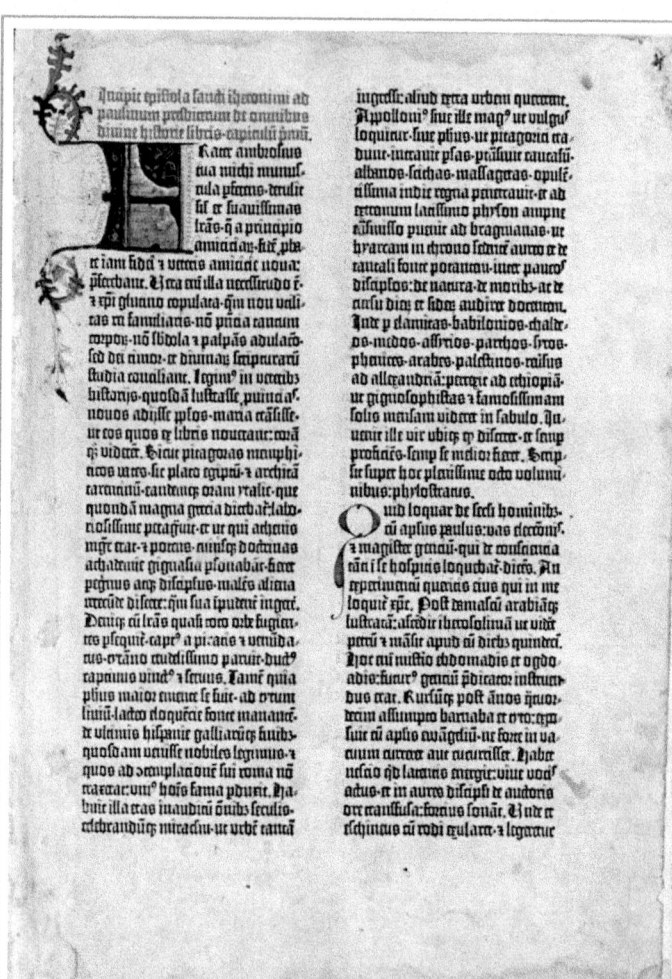

A page from the Gutenberg Bible

What Happened on February 23?

From the creation of great works of engineering and art, to devastating wars and natural disasters, thousands of years of history have left their mark on each and every day of the year. Here are some important events that occurred on February 23. (Items with a photo or illustration are boxed.)

1455 — Traditional date for the publication of the **Gutenberg Bible,** the first mass-produced book in Europe.

1836 — The **Battle of the Alamo** begins when 1,500 Mexican troops arrive in San Antonio. It will last for 13 days before Santa Anna's forces overrun and kill all the defenders.

Fall of the Alamo, Theodore Gentilz (Courtesy Texas State Library)

1861 — Following an alleged assassination plot, President-elect **Abraham Lincoln secretly arrives in Washington,** DC.

1898 — Influential French writer **Émile Zola is found guilty of libel for his open letter** "J'Accuse...!" accusing the French government of anti-Semitism and unlawful conduct in the imprisonment of Alfred Dreyfus, and subsequently flees to England to avoid imprisonment.

1905 — The **Rotary Club**, the first international service organization, is founded.

1927 — Nobel Prize-winning physicist **Werner Heisenberg** first describes his groundbreaking **"uncertainty principle"** in a letter to fellow physicist Wolfgang Pauli.

1942 — In the **first shelling of the North American mainland** during World War II, a Japanese submarine fires on US coastal targets near Santa Barbara, California. Although damage is minimal, it triggers an invasion scare and influences the decision to intern Japanese-Americans for the duration of the war. (The Steven Spielberg film *1941* is loosely based on this event.)

"J'Accuse...!" by Émile Zola, front page of *L'Aurore*, January 13, 1898

Quote of the Day

"Nothing ever becomes real till it is experienced — Even a proverb is no proverb to you till your life has illustrated it."

John Keats, poet
died February 23, 1821

Births
and
Deaths

February 23

W. E. B. Du Bois (Photo: Addison N. Scurlock).

Notable February 23 People

With the current world population at about seven billion people, on average about 19 million people also celebrate their birthdays on February 23 — and that isn't counting millions and millions who came before! No matter when you were born, you share your birthday with many special people whose accomplishments (and occasionally embarrassments) have been noted as part of history.

In this section, you'll meet fascinating people who share your birthday. They're organized by what they're famous for, and then in reverse chronological order from most recent to earliest. Those who are shown in photographs or artwork have a box around them. We don't have photos of everyone, so please forgive us if your favorite person is missing.

Some of these people you've heard of, others will be new to you, but they all make up an important part of the reason that February 23 is a truly special day!

Paul Tibbets, pilot of the B-29 *Enola Gay* (now on display at the Udvar-Hazy Center, Smithsonian National Air and Space Museum) waves from the cockpit prior to his departure to drop the first atomic bomb on Hiroshima. Paul Tibbets was born February 23, 1915. (Photo: PFC Armen Shamalian)

Who Was Born on February 23?

Business

Michael Dell, founder and CEO of computer maker Dell, Inc. *(1965)*

César Ritz, known as the "king of hoteliers," built the Ritz Hotel chain, giving rise to the phrase "Puttin' on the Ritz" and the term "ritzy." *(1850)*

Mayer Amschel Rothschild, created the Rothschild banking dynasty, known as "the founding father of international finance." *(1744)*

Civil Rights

W. E. B. Du Bois, one of the most important figures in the American Civil Rights movement, a of the co-founders of the NAACP. His many books include *The Souls of Black Folk* and *Black Reconstruction in America.* *(1868)*   *(Photo page 14)*

Government

Crown Prince Naruhito (皇太子徳仁親王**),** heir apparent to the Chrysanthemum Throne of Japan. *(1960)*

Letters

Bernard Cornwell, historical novelist best known for his novels about Napoleonic Wars rifleman Richard Sharpe. *(1944)*

William Shirer, journalist and historian known for *The Rise and Fall of the Third Reich. (1904)*

Erich Käster, author of the children's book *Emil and the Detectives*, adapted into film five times, including a 1964 Walt Disney version. *(1899)*

Samuel Pepys, British government official and member of Parliament called "the greatest diarist of all time" for his highly detailed and frank *The Diary of Samuel Pepys*, which was first published in 1825, over a century after his death. *(1633)*

Military

Paul Tibbets, pilot of the B-29 **Enola Gay** (named for his mother) that dropped the atomic bomb on the city of Hiroshima. *(1915) (Photo page 16)*

Music

Robert Lopez, songwriter for such Broadway hits as *The Book of Mormon* and *Avenue Q*; composed the songs for the Disney film *Frozen*; youngest person to ever win an Emmy, Grammy, Oscar and Tony Award. *(1975)*

Samuel Pepys, by John Hayls (1666)

Georg Frideric Händel (engraving by J. Faber, 1749)

Brad Whitford, best known as the rhythm guitarist for the rock band Aerosmith. *(1952)*

Johnny Winter, blues and rock musician and producer, member of the Blues Foundation Hall of Fame and of the *Rolling Stone* magazine list of the 100 Greatest Guitarists of All Time. *(1944)*

Georg Frideric Händel, German baroque composer who spent most of his career in London, known for such works as *The Messiah, Water Music, and Music for the Royal Fireworks. (1685 O.S. [N.S. March 5])*

Performing Arts

Dakota Fanning, actress in such films as *War of the Worlds, Charlotte's Web,* and *Coraline;* youngest Screen Actors Guild Award nominee in history for her debut in 2001's *I Am Sam* at age seven. *(1994)*

Emily Blunt, actress known for her roles in such films as *The Devil Wears Prada, The Young Victoria, The Adjustment Bureau,* and *The Girl on the Train. (1983)*

Aziz Ansari, actor and comedian best known as Tom Haverford on the 2009-2015 sitcom *Parks and Recreation. (1983)*

Kelly Macdonald, Scottish actress who appeared in *Trainspotting, Gosford Park, Harry Potter and the Deathly Hallows — Part 2,* and *No Country for Old Men;* nominated for an Emmy for her role in the television series *Boardwalk Empire.* (1976)

Patricia Richardson, actress best known as the wife of the lead character on the 1990s sitcom *Home Improvement.* (1951)

Peter Fonda, best known for his 1968 film *Easy Rider*, son of actor Henry Fonda and sister of Jane Fonda. *(1940)*

Diane Varsi, nominated for an Academy Award for her debut film performance in the 1957 film *Peyton Place,* also known for her role in the cult classic *Wild in the Streets.* (1938)

Majel Barrett, actress best known as Nurse Chapel in the original *Star Trek* series, wife of series creator Gene Roddenberry. (1932)

Terence Fisher, horror film director best known for his work for Hammer Films, beginning with 1957's *The Curse of Frankenstein.* (1904)

Norman Taurog, filmmaker who became the youngest director ever to win an Academy Award, directed over 180 films. *(1899)*

Victor Fleming, filmmaker best known for *The Wizard of Oz* and *Gone With the Wind.* (1889)

Science

Allan McLeod Cormack, shared the 1979 Nobel Prize in Physiology or Medicine for developing the theories that led to the invention of the CT scanner. *(1924)*

An early poster for the 1968 film *Easy Rider.* From left to right: Dennis Hopper, **Peter Fonda,** Jack Nicholson.

Sports

Joe-Max Moore, American soccer forward, elected to the US Soccer Hall of Fame in 2013. *(1971)*

Michael Campbell, Maori golfer from New Zealand who won the US Open and the £1,000,000 HSBC World Match Play Championship in 2005. *(1969)*

Steve Stricker, American golfer who reached No. 2 in the Official World Golf rankings. (1967)

Fred Biletnikoff, NFL wide receiver for the Oakland Raiders, member of both the college and pro Football Halls of Fame. *(1943)*

Tom Osborne, one of the most successful coaches in American college football history, member of the College Football Hall of Fame, later a member of the US House of Representatives. *(1937)*

Elston Howard, baseball catcher and left fielder, first African-American to play for the New York Yankees, named MVP in the American League. *(1929)*

Elston Howard (Photo: Arnie Lee, CC BY-SA 3.0)

John Keats, by William Hilton the Younger

Who Died on February 23?

Business

John Robert Gregg, invented Gregg Shorthand and published the *Gregg Manual of Style*. *(1848)*

Government

José Napoleón Duarte, President of El Salvador during the Salvadoran Civil War. *(1990)*

John Quincy Adams, 6th President of the United States, son of 2nd President John Adams. *(1848)*

Letters

Robert K. Merton, sociologist and writer awarded the National Medal of Science, developed the terms "role model," "self-fulfilling prophecy," and "unintended consequences." *(2003)*

James Herriot, veterinary surgeon in Yorkshire, England, best known for his semi-autobiographical animal stories, beginning with 1972's *All Creatures Great and Small*. *(1995)*

John Keats, English romantic poet whose famous works include "Ode on a Grecian Urn," "On First Looking Into Chapman's Homer," and "La Belle Dame sans Merci." *(1821)*

Military

Tomoyuki Yamashita (山下 奉文), Japanese World War II general known as the "Tiger of Malaya" for his accomplishment of conquering Malaya and Singapore in only 70 days, called by Winston Churchill the "worst disaster" and "largest capitulation" in British military history. *(1946)*

Horst Wessel, early member of the Nazi Party, portrayed as a martyr to the cause and used as a propaganda symbol following his murder by members of the Communist Party. Known for writing the lyrics for "*Die Fahne Hoch,*" (Raise the Flag) which became a Nazi anthem known as the "*Horst-Wessel-Lied,*" or Horst Wessel Song. It's the song that the Nazi officers sing in Rick's Café Américain in the 1942 film *Casablanca. (1930)*

Music

Harry Ruby, composer known for such songs as "A Kiss to Build a Dream On," "I Wanna Be Loved By You," "Three Little Words," and "Who's Sorry Now." He also wrote numerous songs for Marx Brothers films, including *Duck Soup* and *Horsefeathers.* (1974)

Edward Elgar, English composer who wrote the *Pomp and Circumstance March*, often played during graduation ceremonies. *(1934)*

General Tomoyuki Yamashita surrenders to US forces (1945)

Performing Arts

Madhubala, Indian actress known as the "Marilyn Monroe of Bollywood." *(1969)*

Stan Laurel, comedian, actor, and director, famous as part of the comedy duo Laurel and Hardy. *(1965)*

Science and Medicine

Dickinson W. Richards, shared the 1956 Nobel Prize in Physiology or Medicine for developing the technique of cardiac catheterization. *(1973)*

Leo Baekeland, chemist known as the "father of the plastics industry" for his invention of Bakelite. *(1944)*

Carl Friedrich Gauss, Influential German mathematician known as the *princeps mathematicorum* ("foremost of mathematicians"). *(1855)*

Sports

Sir Stanley Matthews, English footballer (soccer player) considered one of the best of all time, only player to have been knighted while still playing, known as the "wizard of the dribble." *(2000)*

Stan Laurel (left) with Oliver Hardy in the 1939 film *The Flying Deuces* (RKO)

Quote of the Day

"To believe all men honest would be folly. To believe none so is something worse. "

John Quincy Adams, 6th President of the United States, died February 23, 1848

Holidays
Around
the World

February 23

"The Feast Before the Altar of Terminus" (Giovanni Benedetto Castiglione, circa 1842) — for the Roman festival of TERMINALIA

Holidays Around the World

If you're looking for a reason to take your special day off, you should know that every single day is a holiday somewhere in the world! Here's some of what you can celebrate on February 23!

General Events

Mashramani (Guyana)

The South American nation of Guyana became a republic on February 23, 1970. It is celebrated in a festival known as *Mashramani* (or just "Mash,"), which translates as "the celebration after hard work." *(Always February 23)*

Hari Kebangsaan (Brunei)

The Southeast Asian nation of Brunei celebrates its independence as National Day, or *Hari Kebansaan*. *(Always February 23)*

День защитника Отечества (Russia and other former Soviet states)

Formerly known as Red Army Day in the Soviet Union, February 23 is now celebrated as Defender of the Fatherland Day in Russia and a number of other nations that had been part of the Soviet Union. It is celebrated with parades, speeches, and laying a wreath on the Tomb of the Unknown Soldier at the Kremlin. *(February 23 except in Kazakhstan, where it is celebrated on May 7)*

Terminalia (ancient Rome)
The Roman festival of Terminalia honored the god of boundaries, Terminus. In addition to a feast and sacrifices, property owners would mark the boundaries of their land with stones. In those days, February 23 was the last day of the year, so Terminalia also terminated the old year. *(Always February 23) (image page 34)*

Food Holidays

In the United States, almost every day of the year is dedicated to a particular food. (Some other countries also have official food days, but only in America is there one every single day!) Sponsored by manufacturers, retailers, farmers, or simply fans, these days are often proclaimed by the President, Congress, state governors, or mayors. Given that there are more different foods than days of the year, some days honor more than one kind of food!

In the US, February 23 is **National Banana Bread Day**. Bananas first became available in the US in the 1870s, but it wasn't until 1933 that an official banana bread recipe first appeared in print. Bananas were still quite expensive at the time, so nobody wanted to throw away overripe bananas. This way, they could become a new tasty treat!

In addition, the entire month of February is used to celebrate numerous foods. Here's a list of what to eat in the month of February!

- Canned Food Month
- National Chocolate Lovers Month
- National Cherry Month
- National Grapefruit Month
- National Snack Food Month
- National Potato Lovers Month

- Return Shopping Carts to the Supermarket Month

- National Hot Breakfast Month

An abandoned shopping cart, by Michiel1972 (CC BY-SA 3.0) for
RETURN SHOPPING CARTS TO THE SUPERMARKET MONTH

Religious Feast Days and Holidays

Ash Wednesday/Shrove Tuesday

The Lenten season prior to Easter has events that sometimes fall on February 23. In the Netherlands, Shrove Tuesday is celebrated as **National Pancake Day**. In Latvia, the festival of **Meteņi** ends on Ash Wednesday. Of course, Shrove Tuesday is also the occasion of **Mardi Gras.**

Mardi Gras

French for "Fat Tuesday," this celebration takes place the day before Ash Wednesday, the beginning of the Lenten season. The New Orleans Mardi Gras celebration is perhaps the most famous, but Mardi Gras and the Carnival season (between Ephiphany and Ash Wednesday) are celebrated in many areas with large Catholic populations. It's known as *Karneval* or *Fasching* in Germany, *Martedi Grasso* in Italy, and *Fettisdagen* in Sweden.

Mardi Gras can take place anywhere from February 3 to March 9 in regular years, and from February 4 to March 9 in leap years.

Lent

Ash Wednesday begins the season of Lent, a period of prayer and self-denial commemorating the 40 days Jesus spent fasting in the desert, can begin any day between February 4 and March 10 in common years, and as late as March 11 in leap years. The exact beginning of Lent is calculated differently by different Christian denominations.

Sheet music for the "Mardi Gras Rag," 1914

Saint Days

Each day in the year is considered a feast day for one or more saints. They are somewhat different in western Christianity (Catholicism and many forms of Protestantism) and in eastern (Orthodox) Christianity. There are many others; this is a selection.

In *Western Christianity*, it is the feast day of Saints Polycarp of Smyrna and Serenus the Gardener.

In *Eastern Orthodox Christianity*, it is also the commemoration of Saints John Theristes the Harvester, Martha, Romana, Florentius of Seville, Felix of Brescia, Boswell of Scotland, Mildburga, Medrald, and Willigis. (These saints are honored on February 10 by "Old Calendrists.")

Honorary Months

Presidents, Congresses, and nations around the world issue proclamations recognizing particular months to honor certain causes. These events generally fall in February, though honorary months do come and go. Holidays established by states and nonprofit organizations are listed if verified. If not otherwise specified, all months are US. There is some variation from year to year; some celebratory months get added and others get dropped. Two places to get up to date information are the current edition of *Chase's Calendar of Events* or the website Brownielocks. Here are some honorary designations for February.

Black History Month (United States, Canada)

One of the most famous honorary months is Black History Month (sometimes African-American History Month). During Black History Month, important people and events in the African diaspora are commemorated. In the US and Canada, Black History Month is observed in February; in the UK, it's October.

"The First Vote," by Alfred Waud (1867)

Other honorary month designations for February include:

- American Heart Month
- Grapefruit Month
- International Month of Black Women in the Arts
- International Prenatal Infection Prevention Month
- LGBT History Month (United Kingdom)
- Library Lovers Month
- Marijuana Awareness Month
- National Bird-Feeding Month
- National Cherry Month
- National Condom Month
- National Children's Dental Health Month
- National Haiku Writing Month
- Pet Dental Health Month
- Season for Nonviolence (January 30-April 4, worldwide)
- Spunky Old Broads Month
- Youth Leadership Month

Moveable and Multi-Day Events

Some events take place over a specific week or time period. Start and finish dates may vary from year to year. Some events occur on different days each year (such as "fourth Saturday of a month"). These events sometimes take place on February 23.

Last Tuesday (February 22-29)
- Yukon Heritage Day (Canada)

Last Friday (February 22-29)
- International Stand Up to Bullying Day

Last Saturday (February 22-29)
- Open That Bottle Night

Week Including February 22 (begins February 16-22)
- National Engineers Week (United States)

Just for Fun

Anybody can make up a holiday, and many people do! While none of these are officially recognized and some may come and go, here are a few more holidays for February 23.

- Curling is Cool Day (promoting the sport)

- Diesel Engine Day
- Iwo Jima Day
- National Dog Biscuit Day

"The Curlers," Roger Griffith — for CURLING IS COOL DAY

Quote of the Day

"The most serious charge which can be brought against New England is not Puritanism but February."

Joseph Wood Krutch, critic,
in *The Twelve Seasons* (1949)

About
the
Month
of

THERIACA MAGNA

February

"February," from the *Brevarium Grimani* by Simon Bening (c.1510)

February: The Second Month

The February sunshine steeps your boughs
And tints the buds and swells the leaves within.

— *William Cullen Bryant, "Among the Trees"*

The month of February takes its name from the Latin word *februum*, meaning purification, because the traditional Roman festival Februa, involving ritual purification, took place in what we now know as mid-February each year.

Because the Romans considered winter to be a monthless period, neither January nor February existed in the Roman calendar until 713 BCE, and when February did become a month, it was the last month of the year!

The number of days in February also varied in ancient times because the calendar had to be periodically adjusted to stay in line with the seasons. In some years, it was only 23 days long. When the calendar and the seasons got too far out of alignment, the Romans added a bonus month, called Intercalaris, consisting of 27 days, to bring everything back on track.

Our modern month of February begins with the calendar reforms of Julius Caesar, known as the Julian calendar. (See "On Names and Dates" for more details.) February became 28 days long, with an extra "leap day" added every four years.

Although the Julian calendar remained stable for a long time, it wasn't perfectly accurate, and the calendar gradually drifted away from the seasons again.

In 1582, under Pope Gregory XIII, the Julian calendar gave way to the Gregorian calendar, still in use today. One of the Gregorian reforms was to eliminate Leap Year when a new century was not divisible by four. As a result, 1800 and 1900 were leap years, but 2000 was not.

Although the pronunciation "feb-roo-err-ee" is preferred, the common pronunciation "feb-ew-err-ee" (as if the month was spelled "Feb-u-ary") is acceptable as well.

From the point of view of meteorologists, February is the third month of winter in the northern hemisphere and the third month of summer in the southern hemisphere.

February always starts on the same day of the week as March and November in common years, and on the same day as August in leap years. It ends on the same weekday as October in all years, and in common years also ends on the same weekday as January. In leap years, February is the only month that ends on the same day of the week as it began.

Because February is the only month with 28 days in common years, it is the only month that can pass without a single full moon. This happened in 1999 and will happen again in 2018. It is also the only month (in common years) that can have exactly four full 7-day weeks. This happens once every six years and twice every eleven years.

"February," by Joachim von Sandrart

February in Other Cultures

The month of February has different names in different languages. Some nations use calendars other than the Gregorian, and their months may overlap with February. In lunar-based calendars, such as the Islamic calendar, months move through the seasons. Still, many languages often have a word for February itself.

Albanian: Shkurt
Anglo-Saxon: Sol-monath (cake month)
Arabic (Egypt, Sudan, Yemen): يونأغينافبراير (fibrāyir)
Arabic (Levant): حزيركانوشباط (shubāṭ)
Arabic (Libya): الصهناالنوار (an-nuwwār)
Arabic (Algeria and Tunisia): جأيفيفري (Fīfrī)
Arabic (Morocco): غينافبراير (fibrāyər)
Azerbaijani: Fevral
Basque: Otsail
Bulgarian: февруари (fevruari)
Chinese: 二月 (Cantonese: yihyuht; Mandarin: èryuè; Taiwanese: ji-goeh)
Corsican: Ferraghju
Croatian: Veljačaj
Czech: únor (month of submerging)
Finnish: Helmikuu (month of the pearl)
French: Février
German/Danish/Norwegian/Slovenian: Februar
Greek: Φεβρουάριος (Februoários)
Haitian Creole: Fevriye

Hebrew: ינפברואר (febrû'ar)
Hindi: फ़रवरी (farvarī)
Hungarian: Február
Irish (Gaelic): Feabhra mí Feabhra
Italian: Febbraio
Japanese (traditional calendar): 二月 (nigatsu); 如月(kisaragi)
Kazakh: Ақпан (Aḳpan)
Korean: 이월 (iweol)
Lithuanian: Vasaris
Maori: Hui tanguru
Old English: Solmōnaþ (mud month); Kale-monath (cabbage month)
Polish: Luty (month of ice)
Portuguese: Fevereiro
Russian: февраль (fevrali)
Scottish Gaelic: an Gearran
Sesotho: Hlakola
Spanish: Febrero
Swahili/Dutch/Swedish: Februari
Swazi: iNdlovana
Thai: Kumphaphan
Turkish: şubat
Ukrainian: лютий (ljutyj) (month of hard frost)
Vietnamese: 腆㐰 (tháng ha)
Walloon: Fevrî
Welsh: Chwefror
Yiddish: פֿעברואַר (februar)
Zulu: uFebruwari

October Sayings and Superstitions

Here are some sayings and superstitions associated with the month of February.

February Weather Superstitions

February 12 to 14 were said to be "borrowed" from January. If those days were stormy, the year would have good weather, but if they were clear, the rest of the year would be foul.

When the cat lies in the sun in February / She will creep behind the stove in March.

Of all the months of the year / Curse a fair February.

If it thunders in February, it will frost in April.

If February give much snow / A fine summer it doth foreshow

February Wedding Superstitions

A February bride will be an affectionate wife / And a tender mother.

Married in February's sleepy weather / Life you'll tread in time together.

When February birds do mate / You wed nor dread your fate.

In Morocco, there is a ban on marriage during the seven days of *hesoum* (February 24 to March 4)

Valentine's Day Superstitions

The first man an unmarried woman sees on February 14 will be her future husband.

On Valentine's Day, if a girl writes all the names of her suitors on paper, wraps them in clay, and puts them in water, the piece that rises to the top first is the name of her husband to be.

If a woman sees a robin flying overhead on Valentine's Day, she will marry a sailor. If she sees a sparrow, she will marry a poor man but be very happy. If she sees a goldfinch, she will marry a rich person (happiness not guaranteed).

Leap Year Superstitions

Traditionally, women can propose to men on leap days, because the day had no legal status and therefor traditions did not apply. At one time, there was a Scottish law forbidding a man to refuse such a proposal. To ensure success, women should wear a red petticoat under their dress—and make sure it's partially visible to the man when they propose.

In some European countries, if a man refuses a woman's proposal on February 29, he must buy her 12 pairs of gloves.

In Scotland, it's considered unlucky to be born on a Leap Year's Day. Greeks consider it unlucky to be married during a leap year, and especially on a leap day. If you divorce during a leap year, you will never find happiness again.

February Symbols

Birthstone: Amethyst, representing piety, humility, spiritual wisdom, and sincerity

Birth Flowers: Violet and Primrose

Soviet postage stamp of an amethyst from the 1963 "Precious Stone of the Urals" series

Violet (Photo: Andrew Bossi CC BY-SA 2.5)

Still life (primroses, pears, and pomegranates),
by Henri Fantin-Latour

"February," by Eugène Grasset

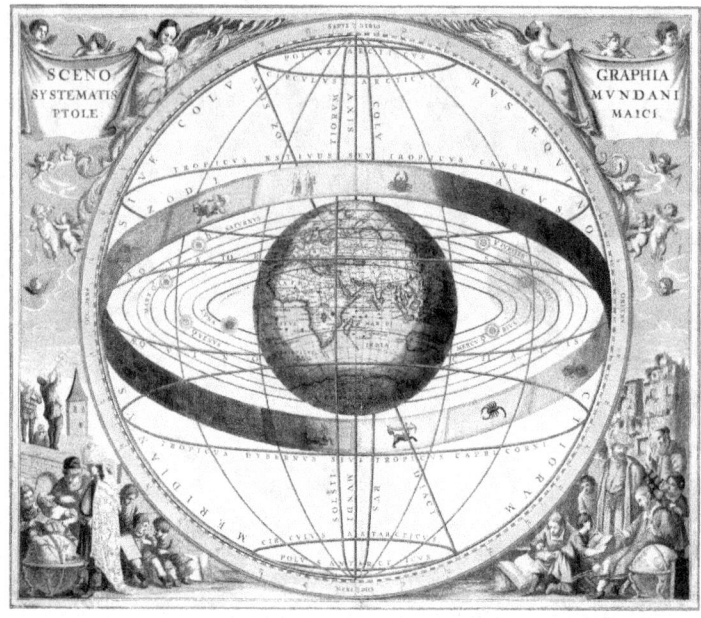

Scenography of the Ptolemaic Cosmography, by Johannes van
Loon, based on Andreas Cellarius's *Harmonia Macrocosmica*, 1660

February 23 Zodiac Signs

From the perspective of someone on Earth, the Sun appears to move through the sky throughout the year, along a path astronomers call the *ecliptic plane*. The ecliptic plane is divided into twelve constellations, known as the zodiac, based on traditionally observed patterns of stars. On your birthday, you can't see your constellation, because it's in the daytime sky.

The zodiac was first developed by Babylonian astronomers about 2,500 years ago. Because they were unaware that the Earth wobbles like a spinning top (known as *precession*), they didn't make allowance for the fact that the Sun's path through the zodiac changes over time.

That means there are now two sets of dates for your birth sign. The *tropical dates* are the original Babylonian dates; the *sidereal dates* tell you where the Sun actually appears as it moves along its annual path.

For October 25, the tropical sign is **Pisces** and the sidereal sign is **Aquarius.**

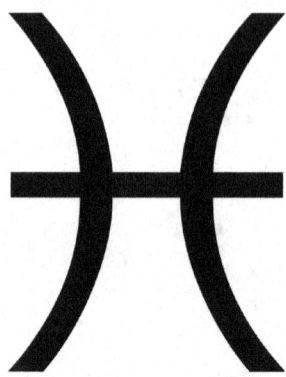

Pisces

Tropical February 20 to March 20
Sidereal March 15 to April 14

In the Roman legend of Venus and her son Cupid, they escaped the clutches of Typhon, known as the "father of all monsters," by transforming into fish and tying themselves together with rope. That's why the name Pisces is plural for fish. The constellation appears as a somewhat ragged "V" shape, representing the rope, with the "fish" located at the two rope ends.

In astrology, Pisces is a water sign, compatible with the other water signs Cancer and Scorpio, as well as with the earth signs Taurus, Virgo, and Capricorn. Pisceans are supposed to be imaginative, compassionate, unworldly, secretive, and escapist.

Aquarius

Tropical January 20 to February 19
Sidereal February 12 to March 8 (March 9 in leap years)

Aquarius is one of the oldest recognized constellations, originally representing the Babylonian god Ea. In Latin, Aquarius means "water-carrier," represented in its symbol. In Greek mythology, Aquarius is sometimes associated with Deucalion, who survived a world-cleansing flood. In Chinese astronomy, it is known as the Black Tortoise of the North (北方玄武, Běi Fāng Xuán Wǔ).

In astrology, Aquarius is considered to be masculine and extroverted, and despite the name is an air sign. Aquarians are supposed to be philanthropical, inventive, and individualistic.

Illustration by Edward Penfield

What Day of the Week is February 23?

On what day of the week does February 23 fall?

Surprisingly, this isn't an easy question. Because the calendar year is 365 days long (366 in leap years), it doesn't divide evenly by the seven days of the week.

Also, the Earth goes around the Sun in about 365-1/4 days, so a calendar tends to drift over time. That's why the same date falls on different weekdays in different years.

This is made even more complicated by a change in calendars that took place in 1582. Our modern calendar has its roots in ancient Rome, in a calendar reform conducted by Julius Caesar. Caesar commissioned mathematicians to attack the problem, and they came up with the idea of leap years, and thus standardized the calendar for centuries to come. This was called the Julian calendar.

Over time, however, the small errors in Caesar's calculation compounded. That's why Pope Gregory XIII commissioned the Gregorian calendar, used in most of the world today. Some countries converted in 1582, when the calendar was first developed; some converted later; other still haven't changed.

Gregorian and Julian aren't the only types of calendars. The Hebrew year, the Islamic year, and many other calendars are used in different parts of the world and among different people.

You can convert Gregorian dates to other calendars, including the Hebrew calendar, the Islamic calendar, and even the Mayan calendar by visiting the Fourmilab Calendar Converter at http://www.fourmilab.ch/documents/calendar/.

Chinese calendar systems are quite complex and have changed several times; a full discussion is far beyond the scope of this book. If you're interested, you can find information here: http://www.hermetic.ch/cal_stud/chinese_cal.htm.

On Names and Dates

Historians use "CE" (Common Era) and "BCE" (Before the Common Era) instead of the more common "AD" (Anno Domini, or Year of Our Lord) and "BC" (Before Christ), reflecting the fact that the year-numbering system established by the Gregorian calendar is used throughout the world in many countries not culturally Christian.

The CE/BCE designation dates back to at least 1708, and has been adopted as a standard by the United Nations and the Universal Postal Union. Because this series of books covers events and people of all nations and cultures, we use the CE/BCE terms.

The abbreviation "O.S." ("Old Style") and "N.S." ("New Style") on some dates refers to the fact

that the Russian Empire (in particular) did not
switch from the Julian to the Gregorian calendar at
the same time as the rest of Europe, and therefore
some figures and events have two dates.

Also, in the Julian calendar in England in the 16th
century, the year began on March 25 rather than
January 1. To avoid confusion with Gregorian dates,
dates between January and March were often written
using both years.

People and events whose original names are not
in the Western alphabet have their native names
(where possible) in the appropriate script shown in
parenthesis. If you are using an e-reader to access an
electronic version of this book, all characters don't
always display on all devices.

A 50-year brass perpetual calendar.

Quote of the Day

"Time is an illusion, lunchtime doubly so."

Douglas Adams,
from *The Hitchhiker's Guide to the Galaxy*

Notes
and
Credits

Timespinner
Press

Cartoon by John T. McCutcheon

Copyright, Credit, and Contact

Follow Us

Our blog "This Day in History" (http://
timespinnerpress.com/this-day-in-history/) features short
articles on events and people associated with each day, and
updates several times each week. Also subscribe to the
"Quote of the Day" at http://timespinnerpress.com/quote-
of-the-day/. You can get daily links by following us on
Facebook at TimespinnerPress, or on Twitter as
@sidewisethinker.

Contact Us

Find an error or a format problem? Want information about
the series, about us, or about when the volume for your
special day might be available? Please email us at
editor@timespinnerpress.com. (We also take requests if your
special day isn't yet complete. Please give us at least six
weeks' notice if possible.)

Sources

We owe a great debt to Wikipedia, which is our first stop for
research. We attempt to make independent confirmation of
all important dates and facts through a variety of other
sources.

Other sources we frequently use include the Library of
Congress; "on this day" listings from *Encyclopedia Britannica*,
the *New York Times*, and the BBC; Omniglot for the names of
months in other languages; *Chase's Calendar of Events*; and, of
course, the always essential Google.

All art and photographs are either in the public domain, used under a Creative Commons license, or with a "fair use" justification, and most frequently come from Wikimedia Commons and the Library of Congress Prints and Photographs Division.

Attribution is provided where possible, or as requested by the copyright owner, or when there is particular historical significance, listed below. For information about any particular illustration or photograph, please contact us.

Credits

1. The cover photograph of the first Iwo Jima flag raising was taken 23 February 1945 by Marine Corps Staff Sergeant Louis R. Lowery for *Leatherneck* magazine. It is in the public domain as a work created by a member of the US military as part of that person's official duties. The image is available on Wikimedia Commons (as are most illustrations used in this book) as well as from the Library of Congress Prints and Photographs Division, digital ID cph.3c32798.

2. The illustration of the month of February used on the back cover is from the French Gothic illuminated manuscript *Les Très Riches Heures du duc de Berry* by the Limbourg Brothers, Jean Colombe, and an intermediate painter whose name is lost to history. It is in the public domain because its copyright has expired.

3. The box graphic used on the first page is from a 1916 pamphlet entitled "Divorce versus Democracy" authored by G. K. Chesterton, originally published in London by the Society of St. Peter and St. Paul. It is in the public domain in the US because it was published prior to 1923, and is in the public domain in all countries (including the country of origin) in which the copyright time is the author's life plus 70 years or less.

4. The graphic design for the section pages in this book is from a design originally created for a pharmacy label. It is courtesy of Wellcome Images (ICV No 11073, photo V0010813), and is used here under CC BY-SA 4.0.

5. The photograph of the US flag on Mount Suribachi was taken by Coast Guard Photographer's Mate 3rd Class John Papsun, and is courtesy of Defense Imagery, HD-SN-99-02881. It is in the public domain as a work of a member of the US military taken as part of that person's official duties.

6. The photograph of Marines climbing Mount Suribachi is in the public domain as a work of a member of the US military taken as part of that person's official duties. The photographer is unknown.

7. The photograph "Raising the Flag on Iwo Jima" by Joe Rosenthal is copyrighted by the Associated Press, and is not in the public domain. It is used here under "fair use" provisions of the copyright code. The photograph is used to illustrate an educational discussion of its own creation, and therefore no free alternative is available. It is also of low resolution and unsuitable for the creation of counterfeit goods or other commercial works. No challenge to the copyright holder is intended or implied.

8. The outline of the figures at the flag raising on Iwo Jima was created in 2008 by Jeff Dahl, and is used here under CC BY-SA 4.0 and earlier versions of that license.

9. The poster for the 7th War Loan drive is in the public domain as a work created by employees of the US Department of the Treasury.

10. The photograph "A U.S. Marine Corps ceremonial bugler plays taps as an honor guard presents the colors at the Marine Corps War Memorial in Arlington, Va." was taken by Lance Corporal Tia Dufour. It is in the public domain as a work created by a member of the US military as part of that person's official duties. It has been cropped.

11. The page from the Gutenberg Bible was scanned at the Ransom Center of the University of Texas at Austin. It is in the public domain because its copyright has expired.

12. The 1844 painting *Fall of the Alamo* by Theodore Gentilz is in the public domain because its copyright has expired. It is in the collection of the Texas State Library.

13. The front page of the 13 January 1898 issue of the French newspaper *L'Aurore* featuring the letter "J'accuse...!" by

Émile Zola is in the public domain because its copyright has expired.

14. The photograph of W. E. B. Du Bois was taken circa 1911 by Addison N. Scurlock, and is in the collection of the National Portrait Gallery, Washington, DC, accession number NPG 92.1 6-23-94 RW. It is in the public domain because its copyright has expired.

15. The 1945 photograph of Col. Paul Tibbets waving from the cockpit of the atomic bomber *Enola Gay* was taken by PFC Armen Shamlian. It is in the public domain as a work created by a US Army soldier as part of that person's official duties. It is from the collection of the US National Archives, NWDS-208-LU-13H-5.

16. The 1666 painting of Samuel Pepys is by John Hayls. It is in the public domain because its copyright has expired.

17. The 1749 engraving of Georg Frideric Händel is by J. Faber, after a painting by Hudson. It originally appeared in the 1885 publication *Die Gartenlaube*. It is in the public domain because its copyright has expired.

18. The poster for the 1968 film *Easy Rider* is in the public domain because it was first published in the United States between 1923 and 1977 and without a copyright notice.

19. The1965 photograph of Elston Howard was taken by Arnie Lee. It is used here under CC BY-SA 3.0.

20. The 1822 portrait of John Keats is by William Hilton the Younger. It is in the public domain because its copyright has expired.

21. The photograph "General Yamashita and his staff walk down the trail to U.S. forces in northern Luzon" was taken by a photographer from the US Signal Corps on September 2, 1945. It is in the collection of the US National Archives, and is in the public domain as a work created by a US Army soldier or employee as part of that person's official duties.

22. The cropped screenshot from the 1939 RKO film *The Flying Deuces* is in the public domain because it was published in the United States between 1923 and 1963 and although there may or may not have been a copyright notice, the copyright was not renewed.

23. The print "The Feast Before the Altar of Terminus" was created circa 1642 by Giovanni Benedetto Castiglione, and is in the collection of the Harvard Art Museums. It is in the public domain because its copyright has expired.

24. The sheet music cover for the 1914 song "Mardi Gras Rag", by Lyons and Yosco, was published by Geo. W. Meyer Music Co., New York. It is in the public domain because it was first published prior to January 1, 1923.

25. The illustration "The First Vote" by Alfred R. Waud originally appeared on the cover of *Harper's* magazine in 1867. It is in the public domain because its copyright has expired.

26. The 1860 illustration "The Curlers," by Roger Griffith, is in the public domain because its copyright has expired.

27. The painting "February" is from the *Brevarium Grimani,* circa 1510, and is in the public domain because its copyright has expired.

28. The painting "February" by Joachim von Sandrart is in the public domain because its copyright has expired. The original can be found in the Staatsgalerie im Neuen Schloss, Schleißheim, Germany.

29. The 1815 woodcut of a proposal is in the public domain because its copyright has expired.

30. The 1896 drawing "February" by Eugène Grasset is in the public domain because its copyright has expired.

31. The 1963 Soviet postage stamp of an amethyst from the "Precious Stones of the Urals" series is not an object of copyright according to article 1259 of Book IV of the Civil Code of the Russian Federation No. 230-FZ, 12/18/2006.

32. The photograph of violets at the Abbey Church of Saint Peter, Salzburg, Austria, was taken by Andrew Bossi and used here under CC BY-SA 2.5.

33. The painting "Nature morte (primevères, poires et grenades)" by Henri Fantin-Latour is in the public domain because its copyright has expired. The original can be found at the Kröller-Müller Museum, Otterlo, Netherlands. Image courtesy Google Art Project by way of Wikimedia Commons.

34. The celestial sphere is from *Scenography of the Ptolemaic Cosmography*, by Johannes van Loon, based on Andreas

Cellarius's *Harmonia Macrocosmica*, 1660. It is in the public domain because its copyright has expired.

35. The 1906 automobile calendar is by Edward Penfield, and is in the collection of the Library of Congress Prints and Photographs Division. It is in the public domain because its copyright has expired.

36. The 50-year perpetual calendar photograph is in the public domain.

37. The cartoon by John T. McCutcheon is from his 1905 collection *The Mysterious Stranger and Other Cartoons by John T. McCutcheon*. It is in the public domain because its copyright has expired.

Timespinner
Press

License Description and Terms

Aside from material purely in the public domain, photographs and other material in this book are used under specific licenses permitting free use, usually with an attribution requirement. For full text and terms of these licenses, click or enter the appropriate links below. If you believe there is an error in the copyright status or attribution of any of these images, please email us.

- Creative Commons Attribution 2.0 Generic (CC-BY 2.0): http://creativecommons.org/licenses/by/2.0/deed.en
- Creative Commons Attribution-Share Alike 3.0 Generic (CC-BY-SA 3.0): http://creativecommons.org/licenses/by-sa/3.0/
- Creative Commons Attribution-Share Alike 2.5 Generic (CC-BY-SA 2.5): http://creativecommons.org/licenses/by-sa/2.5/deed.en
- Creative Commons Attribution-Share Alike 2.0 Generic (CC-BY-SA 2.0): http://creativecommons.org/licenses/by/2.0/deed.en
- Creative Commons Attribution-Share Alike 1.0 Generic (CC-BY-SA 1.0): http://creativecommons.org/licenses/by-sa/1.0/deed.en
- CC0 1.0 Universal (CC0 1.0) Public Domain Dedication (CC0 1.0) http://creativecommons.org/publicdomain/zero/1.0/deed.en
- GNU Free Documentation License (GFDL): http://en.wikipedia.org/wiki/Wikipedia:Text_of_the_GNU_Free_Documentation_License
- License Art Libre (Free Art License): http://artlibre.org

Other Books from Timespinner Press

The Story of a Special Day
Michael Dobson

A series of (eventually) 366 volumes covering everything that happened on your special day! Events, births, deaths, quotes, holidays, and much more. It's like a birthday card they'll never throw away!

US$7.95 print / US$2.99 ebook.

From Plassey to Pakistan
Humayun Mirza

The history of British Colonial India and the formation of Pakistan from the unique perspective of the son of Pakistan's first president and last of the royal line of Bengal, Bihar, and Orissa! This unique historical document tells the inside story of this distinguished family, including the detailed story of the coup that toppled his father from power!

US$27.95 print

A Whole New Navy: America's War in the Pacific

Miles Durr

The most comprehensive and detailed description of America's naval war in the Pacific ever—every battle, every ship, every task force and every task group from Pearl Harbor through the Japanese surrender! A must-have for the collection of every World War II buff!

US$29.95 print

Improbable History: The Weird, the Obscure, and the Strangely Important

edited by Michael Dobson

From the birth of Western civilization to the rescue of Apollo 13, from the Leaning Tower of Pisa to Florence's Duomo, history has often turned on small, improbable details. Whatever happened to the ancient Samaritan people? Why did a fortuitous rainstorm allow the British to conquer India? How did an air raid in Italy lead to the development of chemotherapy? What happened when Albert Einstein met Adolf Hitler on the streets of Berlin? How did the Japanese manage to attack the US mainland using balloons? A cast of award-winning writers tackle some of the strangest tales in history!

US$19.95 print